Vampires

Vampires

monster
Chronicles

STEPHEN KRENSKY

Lerner Publications Company · Minneapolis

Lerner Publications Company
A division of Lerner Publishing Group
241 First Avenue North
Minneapolis, MN 55401 U.S.A.

Website address: www.lernerbooks.com

Library of Congress Cataloging-in-Publication Data

Krensky, Stephen.
    Vampires / by Stephen Krensky.
      p. cm. — (Monster chronicles)
    Includes bibliographical references and index.
    ISBN-13: 978-0-8225-5891-0 (lib. bdg. : alk. paper)
    ISBN-10: 0-8225-5891-2 (lib. bdg. : alk. paper)
    I. Vampires. I. Title. II. Series. Monster chronicles.
  GR830.V3K74 2007
  398′.45—dc22   2005024479

Manufactured in the United States of America
1 2 3 4 5 6 - JR - 12 11 10 09 08 07

TABLE OF CONTENTS

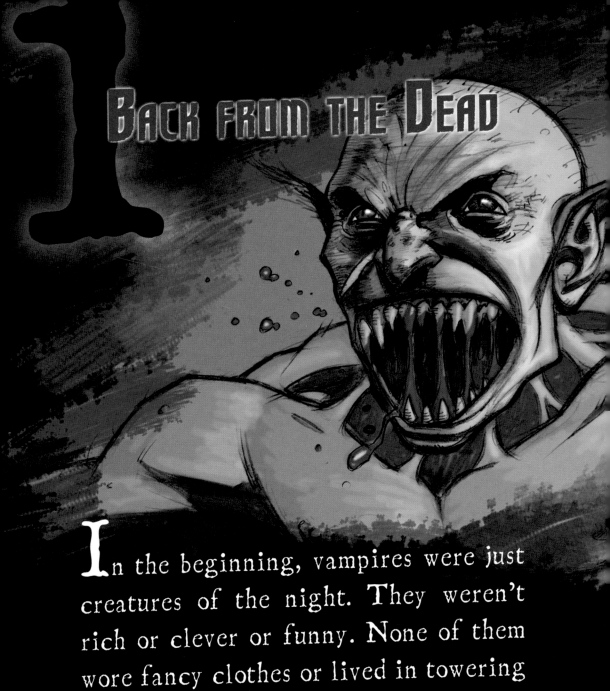

Back from the Dead

In the beginning, vampires were just creatures of the night. They weren't rich or clever or funny. None of them wore fancy clothes or lived in towering castles. Vampires had no friends. They

didn't speak English with foreign accents. In fact, they may not have spoken at all.

But vampires were always evil. There was no confusion about them, none of that Good Witch versus Bad Witch stuff. Vampires didn't wrestle with big moral issues. They didn't wonder about their place in the universe. Once upon a time, if you saw a vampire after dark, you ran for your life (or what little was left of it).

According to the *Oxford English Dictionary*, the word *vampire* first appeared in English in 1734.

Vampires were bad for two big reasons. For one thing, they were dead. And death would make anyone cranky. The second reason was their drinking habits. All vampires—spirits or demons or dead people—

were thirsty for the same thing. Blood. And for some reason, animal blood wasn't good enough. Vampires craved human blood.

They weren't always fussy about whose blood it was. A vampire peasant, for example, might come back from the grave seeking revenge against a cruel nobleman. He couldn't wait to get that nobleman in his clutches. But what if, on the way to the nobleman's castle, the new vampire ran into someone else, someone he didn't even know? Well, he would probably stop for a little snack.

The word *vampire* itself comes from the Slavic word *vampir*. But eastern Europe was not the first place vampires called home. They have inspired countless legends from all over the world. Thousands of years ago, Middle Eastern civilizations such as the Babylonians, the Assyrians, and the Egyptians had vampire tales to relate.

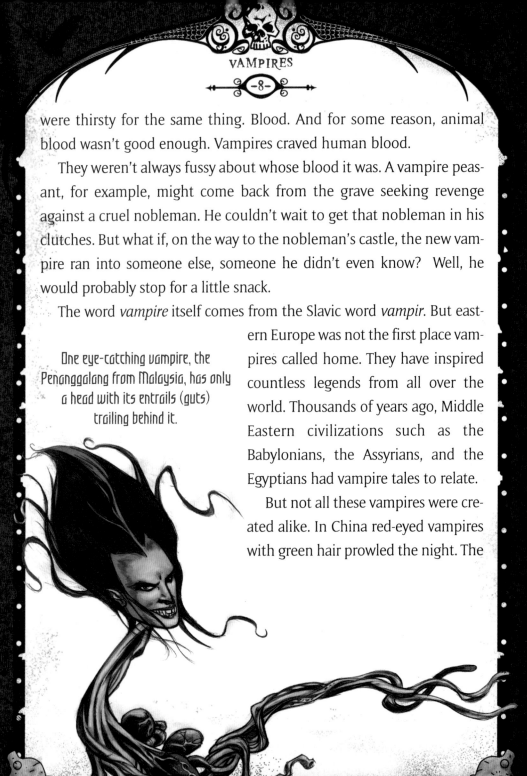

One eye-catching vampire, the Penanggalang from Malaysia, has only a head with its entrails (guts) trailing behind it.

But not all these vampires were created alike. In China red-eyed vampires with green hair prowled the night. The

Indian vampirelike goddess Kali has four arms and prominent fangs and wears a necklace of skulls around her neck. In Greece a vampire was a snakelike creature with a woman's head that stole away children to drink their blood.

Along with her skull necklace, Kali (*above*) wears a belt of arms and carries a severed head. She's a symbol of destruction in Hindu lore, but she also keeps order in the world.

STARTING A BLOOD DRIVE

So why were stories of vampires so widespread? Well, the most important factor was human nature. Like other myths and legends, the idea of vampires helped to explain some mysterious things. How could that seemingly healthy farmer have died in his sleep? It wasn't possible— unless a vampire had gotten to him. And what about that odd fellow

who kept to himself and only seemed to go out at night? That was pretty strange. Such people, it was whispered, had made deals with the devil. Perhaps he was already dead and had risen from the grave. Then, too, like many people accused of witchcraft, mean or unpopular people were tarred as supernatural as an excuse to get rid of them.

Of course, nobody knew exactly when a new vampire would appear. It was a bit unpredictable. If a funeral wasn't handled properly, the dearly departed might come back to complain. Or what if a death seemed sudden or unfair? Then the dead person might choose to leave the grave and roam among the living—making their lives as miserable as possible.

As difficult as a vampire was, though, it could only be in one place at a time. So with luck you could avoid it. But what about two vampires? Or three? It was known that one

Ancient Egyptians took great care of their dead. They wanted their loved ones to be prepared for the afterlife. *Below*, an Egyptian priest wraps a dead body in strips of clean linen.

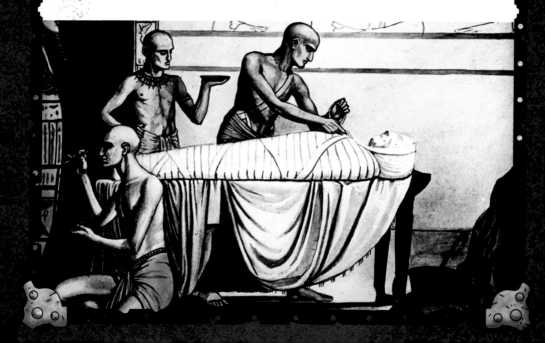

vampire could turn a regular person into another vampire with a few timely bites to the neck. And a single vampire was bound to want company. So if a vampire was in your neighborhood, it was important to stay on your toes.

Fortunately, there are no records of vampires actually taking over a country (much less the world). So we can safely assume vampires are not too successful at spreading themselves around. But no one should get overconfident. Vampires, if they stay out of harm's way, live forever. Even now, they may be biding their time, waiting for the right moment to strike.

In European legend, vampires and graveyards go hand in hand. So it's no surprise that people took great care to avoid cemeteries after dark. You would, too, if you thought a blood-sucking corpse was going to jump out of the grave at you.

Vampires on Parade

So what's a vampire like? Well, they come in all shapes and sizes. Vampires can be men, women, or children. (There are even a few instances of vampire plants and animals.) They can be young

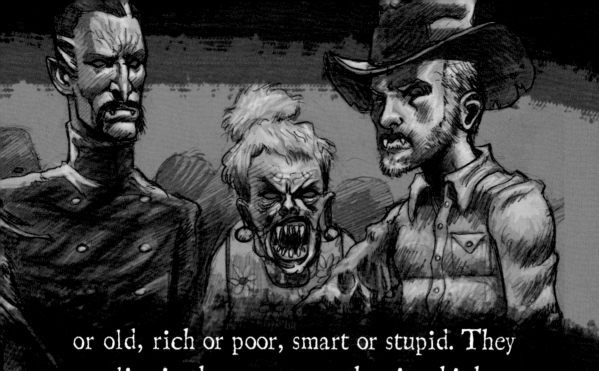

or old, rich or poor, smart or stupid. They can live in the country or the city, high on mountaintops or down in valleys. Some vampires like to travel. Others stay put.

But despite their many differences, vampires have much in common. Start with their pale skin—which makes sense since most of them only come out at night. And that skin is usually cold (vampires not being very warmhearted). Vampires are also unnaturally strong. They have

Vampires cast no shadows, and their reflections don't appear in mirrors. (They're solid enough to the touch, but the light plays tricks on them.)

heightened senses of sight, sound, and smell, so it's hard to catch them by surprise. Many have hypnotic powers, which makes it easier for

them to subdue their victims. And don't forget their extra-long incisor teeth. Those fangs are convenient for sucking out blood.

And there's more. Some vampires can fly. Others are able to change their shape at will. The most common shape seems to be a bat (although the wolf is also popular). A favored few can transform into mists, which comes in handy for sneaking through keyholes or escaping from a raging mob. There are even vampires who can control creatures such as rats and wolves or conjure up stormy weather. (It's bad enough to face an ordinary vampire. Facing one surrounded by thunder and lightning is much worse.)

Blood-sucking bats are only found in Central and South America. When Spanish explorers noticed the bats feeding on chickens and cows, they began calling them vampire bats. Bats and vampires have been linked ever since.

How to Fight Back

Luckily, vampires have their weaknesses too. They cannot enter a place without being invited. Christian crosses give them headaches, and holy water burns them like acid. They avoid garlic, and they cannot cross running water (such as a river). It is not clear that vampires get tired, but they certainly spend a lot of time

In this scene from the 1992 movie *Bram Stoker's Dracula*, a vampire has a bad reaction to a Christian cross.

Some vampires had children called *dhampirs*. Dhampirs were the only people who could see invisible vampires. But the dhampirs were not very loyal to their parents—they often hired themselves out as vampire hunters.

asleep. (And when they're snoozing, of course, they are most vulnerable to attack.)

Still, killing vampires is hard. Conventional weapons are useless. Bullets, arrows, and swords only slow vampires down for a bit (unless they are beheaded in the process). They recover from wounds in minutes or hours instead of weeks or months. Soon they are ready to strike again.

People who are bitten by vampires either die forever or turn into vampires themselves. To stop a vampire, a brave person can drive a wooden stake through the vampire's heart.

But vampires can die. They can be burned by fire. They can be suffocated by stuffing their mouths with dirt from their resting place. Driving a wooden stake through their hearts also finishes them off. Most important of all, sunlight is often fatal, almost instantly frying them to a crisp.

Vampires also have their quirks. One traditional way to outwit them was to spread seeds around their graves. Supposedly, when the vampire rose up at night, the seeds would distract him. He would start counting . . . and counting . . . and counting. He would be so busy counting that he wouldn't get around to terrorizing the countryside. Keep in mind that these were ordinary seeds. The vampires weren't going to eat them or collect them and show them off to their friends. Apparently, it was the counting that mattered. So if the neighbors got really lucky, the vampire wouldn't notice the sun was coming up until it was too late and—POOF!—no more vampire.

> Parents sometimes placed iron shavings beneath their baby's cradle, because vampires don't like iron.

No vampire has all these traits. This makes sense since these attributes come from many places and cultures. Unlike, say, ghosts, who don't vary much from one place to the next, vampires adapt. They're flexible. And while this may be a good thing for vampires—who seem to become more powerful as the centuries pass—it's not such good news for the rest of us.

3 Real-Life Vampires in History

As long as there have been vampires, there have been vampire victims. But in the distant past, news didn't travel too far or too fast. So vampire reports and attacks never got much attention. And they were all

lumped together. Vampires were just one of those things—like the plague—that was better to avoid.

But as communications became more sophisticated, things changed. The founding of newspapers and magazines expanded readers' local horizons. And by the 1700s, better roads and faster sailing ships carried news and information farther than ever before.

Early vampires were not always afraid of sunlight, although they consistently lost their power during the day.

So in 1725, when neighbors destroyed Peter Plogojowitz as a vampire, the word got around. Peter was a Serbian peasant in eastern

Europe who had died at the age of sixty-two. There had been nothing unusual about Peter's death. But for ten weeks after he was buried, different villagers reported seeing him up and about at night. This was unsettling. And Peter wasn't just wandering around—he was attacking villagers in their beds. Supposedly, nine people had already died.

Clearly, Peter had to be stopped. And what better way to stop him than to dig up his body? And what did they find? Signs of a vampire, that's what. Peter's body showed little decomposition, even after three months in the ground. His nose and skin didn't look their best, but it appeared that new skin was growing underneath. His hair and fingernails were growing as well. And there were signs of fresh blood around his mouth.

The villagers had seen enough. Maybe things would have turned out differently if Peter had sat up at that moment to defend himself. (And then again, maybe not.) In any event, the villagers lost no time driving a wooden stake through his heart. And then, just in case, they burned his body too. But was Peter really a vampire? Well, the attacks stopped after that, so it was hard to argue with success.

Two years later, another case got wide attention. Another Serbian, Arnold Paole, who reportedly had been dead for a while, started showing up in people's houses. That was bad enough. But when some of the people Arnold visited

Erszebet Bathory (1560–1614), known as the Blood Countess, reportedly bathed in the blood of young women. She was under the impression that it would keep her young. It didn't. This was too bad for her, but even worse for the young women.

turned up dead, that was worse. Again, villagers dug up his grave. And again, the diggers were not disappointed. Arnold's body was well preserved. Fresh blood was found, along with new skin growing to replace the old. Wasting no time, the villagers drove a stake through his heart. But unlike Peter Plogojowitz, who had suffered his attack in silence, Arnold reportedly groaned.

Modern science could have explained some of what the villagers found. For example, bodies that seemed healthy, not shrunken or shriveled, were actually just bloated with gases created as the body decayed. And fingernails continue to grow after death. But biology—especially concerning dead people—was not well understood in the 1700s. Besides, frightened villagers saw what they wanted or expected to see. And the skeptics kept their mouths shut. Had they spoken out, they could easily have been accused of being vampires themselves.

The sound of Arnold Paole's groan may have come from the release of pent-up gases in his body.

Serbia, of course, was just one country. Soon villagers throughout eastern Europe were also digging up graves and burning suspicious-looking bodies. But people were not sleeping any better. Every bump in the night made them jump. Finally, the Austrian empress Maria Theresa sent her own doctor to check out the different stories. After a thorough investigation, the doctor found no evidence that vampires existed. Maria Theresa then created laws to keep people from opening graves whenever they felt like it. Pretty soon things calmed down again.

An actual blood disorder called porphyria can make some people feel a little like vampires. Porphyria victims avoid the sunlight because their skin is so sensitive to it. Their gums also tend to tighten and recede, making their teeth more prominent.

A New Kind of Immortality

After so much publicity, though, it was only natural that writers should take up the topic of vampires. Among the first works to feature them in English was "The Vampyre," a story published in England in 1819. Its author was John Polidori, but the idea had come from his friend, the poet Lord Byron. Another popular English book, *Varney the Vampyre,* by James Malcolm Rymer, was published in 1847. Varney is not much remembered these days, but he has one definite claim to fame. He apparently was the first vampire to have fangs.

Still, vampires lagged far behind ghosts or witches in the reading public's imagination. Fifty years would pass before that changed, so not even vampires could claim that it happened overnight.

Lord Byron *(above)* created his vampire ideas at a villa in Switzerland in 1819. Among the other guests was his friend Mary Shelley who turned her own ideas into the novel *Frankenstein.*

The Most Famous Name in Vampires

Those fifty years echoed the life of a
London theater manager who wrote books
on the side. His name was Bram Stoker,

Stoker had once had a nightmare about a vampire rising from the grave. Inspired by this, he worked on a story for seven years. In 1897 his new novel was published. He called it *Dracula.*

In Stoker's novel, Dracula is a vampire hundreds of years old. He lives in a castle in Transylvania, a real place that is part of modern-day Romania. Dracula's story is told through diary entries, letters, and newspaper clippings. Among the main characters

Bram Stoker (1847–1912) never got rich for creating Dracula, but at least he stopped having those nightmares.

Vlad Tepes translates to Vlad the Impaler. It's a name he richly deserved.

are two beautiful young women, Lucy Westenra and Mina Murray. Dracula is drawn to them. The men trying to defend Lucy and Mina include Mina's fiancé, Jonathan Harker, and a Dutch professor, Abraham Van Helsing. (Luckily, Van Helsing knows a thing or two about vampires and how to fight them.) The story moves from Transylvania to England and then back to Transylvania for its bloody conclusion.

So where did Dracula come from? Well, there was a real-life Transylvanian figure from the fifteenth century named Vlad Tepes. Vlad's father was a ruler known in Romania as the *dracul* (the dragon). Vlad was therefore the son of the dragon—or Dracula. He was born around 1430. In 1456, a few years after the deaths of his father and older brother, Vlad became a ruler too.

Being one of Vlad's enemies was not healthy. Why? Because he had them all killed. During his six-year reign, Vlad and his soldiers impaled thousands of people on wooden stakes and left them to die. Now Vlad may not have been all bad. He did unify the territory that led to the creation of modern Romania. However, his great cruelty remains his strongest legacy.

Stoker's Count Dracula lived in an isolated castle in Romania. Dark, creepy castles became a staple of vampire movies, such as 1931's *Dracula* (left).

Nothing about Vlad's life hinted of vampires. But his nature and location suited Stoker's needs. So Stoker borrowed the parts that interested him and simply made up the rest. It was a winning combination. The reading public was quickly drawn to this new and mysterious figure.

DRACULA TAKES FLIGHT

Given Stoker's theater connections, it was natural for Dracula to be adapted for the stage. Several productions appeared in the decades following the novel's publication, including a very successful production in New York in 1927.

That production led to Dracula's most famous appearance in motion pictures. Filmmakers had already released three Dracula movies. But the fourth film, made in 1931 and starring Bela Lugosi, made the biggest impression. In Stoker's book, Dracula had been noted for hairy palms, overly long fingernails, and bad breath. In the film, he undergoes a bit of a makeover. Lugosi's Dracula was an elegant aristocrat with a distinctive Hungarian accent.

The movie got mixed reviews, but it was a popular success. And no one questions its influence. It inspired other horror movies (notably *Frankenstein*) as well as many successors, including *Dracula's Daughter, Son of Dracula, House of Dracula, Blood of Dracula, The Return of Dracula, Brides of Dracula, Billy the Kid versus Dracula, Batman Fights Dracula, Dracula Has Risen from the Grave, Dracula vs. Frankenstein, Countess Dracula, Blacula, Old Dracula, Dracula's Dog, Dracula's Last Rites, Dracula's Widow, Bram Stoker's Dracula,* and *Dracula 2000.*

NOSFERATU

Nosferatu (1922) was an early vampire film from
Germany. Its vampire, Count Orlock, or Nosferatu,
was played by Max Schreck *(above)*. Reportedly,
Schreck was an odd guy. For one thing, the cast and
crew never saw him out of full makeup and costume.
He seemed to stay in character all the time, even
when the cameras weren't rolling. His appearance
and behavior led to wild rumors that Schreck actually was a vampire. Whether or not this was true, his
creepy weirdness made *Nosferatu* a classic vampire
movie.

Most famous among Lugosi's successors was Christopher Lee. Beginning in 1958 with *House of Dracula*, Lee starred in seven Dracula films. His portrayal represented an important update to the Dracula image on screen. Changes in film techniques and tastes had made Lugosi's portrayal seem dated. Lee's elegant manner and deep voice prompted chills in a whole new generation of audiences.

George Hamilton's Dracula *(below)* liked the nightlife in New York City in *Dracula: Dead and Loving It* (1995).

SMILING THROUGH THE PAIN

By the 1970s, Dracula had been showcased from a lot of angles but rarely with a sense of humor. Two movies sought to fill this gap—*Love at First Bite* (1979) and *Dracula: Dead and Loving It* (1995). In the first, Count Dracula (George Hamilton) is forced to leave his castle in Transylvania. He comes to New York searching for a bride. Life in the big city takes some getting used to, but since New York is the city that never sleeps, the count has plenty of time to try.

Dracula: Dead and Loving It features Leslie Nielsen as the infamous count. Here Dracula finds himself the victim of physical comedy, sight gags, and slapstick sequences. Nielsen's Dracula crashes into windows and falls down stairs. He still thinks of himself as suave and sophisticated, even if nobody else does. The movie also made fun of the serious and creepy *Bram Stoker's Dracula* (1992), which had come

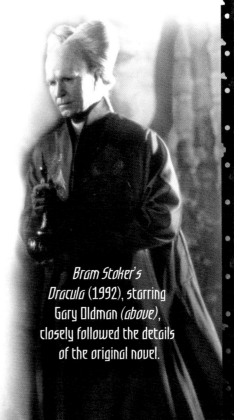

Bram Stoker's Dracula (1992), starring Gary Oldman *(above)*, closely followed the details of the original novel.

Some of the many movie faces of Dracula include Bela Lugosi, Christopher Lee, George Hamilton, Leslie Nielsen, Gary Oldman, and Rudolph Martin.

out three years before. One Dracula making fun of another could get a little confusing, but it certainly proved that Dracula had remained a popular figure for more than a century—especially at a safe distance.

VAMPIRES ON THE LOOSE

Dracula, of course, was not the only vampire who ever lived (or died). In fact, more recent vampires might take offense at the amount of attention he receives. They might also object to being

stereotyped as brooding counts from Transylvania. (Many of them brood, but they live all over.)

One of the more complicated vampires to appear in the media was Barnabas Collins. He was a character in the television soap opera *Dark Shadows.* The series, which premiered in 1966, was set in Collinsport, Maine. Collinsport was a small town but big enough for many supernatural and cemetery plots. Although Barnabas certainly had his vampire needs, he tried to be considerate. Most of his victims did not die—they merely suffered from illnesses, fatigue, and, yes, a loss of blood. Barnabas was also an unusual vampire because he chose to live among ordinary people.

Apparently, Maine is a popular vampire destination. Stephen King's tale of a vampire and his servant terrorizing a small Maine town surfaced

Barnabas Collins (Jonathan Frid) rises from his coffin in *Dark Shadows.* The 1960s afternoon soap opera was close to being cancelled until vampires and ghosts were added to the cast.

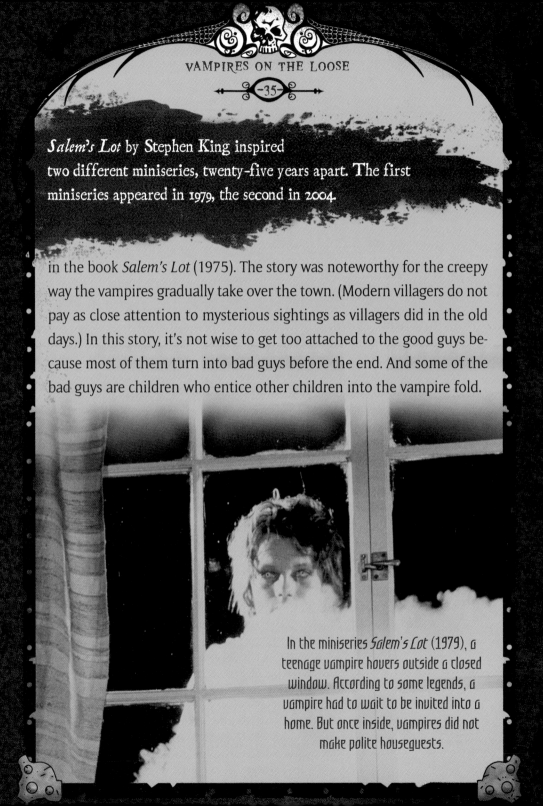

Salem's Lot by Stephen King inspired two different miniseries, twenty-five years apart. The first miniseries appeared in 1979, the second in 2004.

in the book *Salem's Lot* (1975). The story was noteworthy for the creepy way the vampires gradually take over the town. (Modern villagers do not pay as close attention to mysterious sightings as villagers did in the old days.) In this story, it's not wise to get too attached to the good guys because most of them turn into bad guys before the end. And some of the bad guys are children who entice other children into the vampire fold.

In the miniseries *Salem's Lot* (1979), a teenage vampire hovers outside a closed window. According to some legends, a vampire had to wait to be invited into a home. But once inside, vampires did not make polite houseguests.

The vampire invasion of the United States continued with Anne Rice's *Interview with the Vampire* (1976). Set in New Orleans, the book introduced Lestat de Lioncourt, who became one of the best-known vampires of recent years. Rice's vampires are very social, especially among themselves. The action moves across two centuries from New Orleans to Paris to New York, and Rice invigorates the vampire legends with her sense of vampire communities living among us. Her vampires also display a wide range of emotions and attachments. And you know things have changed from Dracula's day when Lestat is awakened from a deep sleep by a rock band rehearsing near his cemetery slumberland.

GETTING AN EARLY START

Anne Rice

Most often, children involved with vampires are simply innocent bystanders caught up in a larger fight. One exception is the movie *The Lost Boys* (a title ironically echoing *Peter Pan*). This 1987 movie focuses on a group of teenage vampires and their interactions with the world. Boys will be boys, but for all their bravado, these teenage vampires still suffer from a strong sense of isolation.

Even the world of younger children has seen vampires cross its threshold. On *Sesame Street*, Count von Count

Actor Tom Cruise has just bitten a victim in *Interview with the Vampire* (1994). Cruise starred as the vampire Lestat in the movie version of Rice's novel.

comes complete with cape, accent, and pointy eyeteeth. He is obsessed with counting (conjuring up memories of ancient vampires counting their seeds). And when he laughs, thunder sounds in the background. He shares his castle home with many bats (which naturally he likes to count too). Count von Count is hardly a threatening figure. But his heritage is clear. The sun has no effect on him, however, leaving him free to enjoy the daylight hours. (Apparently, being a Muppet has its advantages.)

Another addition to the vampire menagerie is the rabbit Bunnicula. He is the title character in the children's book *Bunnicula: A Rabbit Tale of Mystery* by Deborah and James Howe. The Monroe family finds Bunnicula when they attend a showing of the movie *Dracula*. The Monroes name him Bunnicula in honor of the movie. But Chester, the family cat, is suspicious of this black-and-white bunny with the long cape and two pointed teeth. Chester's suspicions only grow when a blood-red tomato in the kitchen turns white (seemingly having had its red color—and life—sucked out of it). "Today, vegetables. Tomorrow . . . the world!" Chester warns Harold, the family dog. It's a sensible warning. Whether or not Bunnicula is a true vampire bunny, Chester keeps a close eye on him—both in this book and in several sequels.

THE VAMPIRE CRAZE CONTINUES

Playing around with vampire lore also lies at the foundation of the film *Buffy the Vampire Slayer* (1992). Buffy is a seemingly empty-headed

Buffy (Kristy Swanson) takes time out from cheer-leading to slay a vampire (below).

The TV version of *Buffy the Vampire Slayer* starred Sarah Michelle Gellar. She tried to keep the vampire population of Sunnydale in check. It was not a job for the fainthearted.

destiny lies not with shopping at the mall but in defeating vampires. She is the Slayer, of which there is only one in each generation.

The humorous friction between Buffy's safe, plastic world and the dark domain of vampires carried over into the television series that followed in 1997. Buffy and her friends had no choice but to take evil se-

On the television show *Angel,* the diabolical law firm
of Wolfram & Hart installed special glass in its office
building to protect vampires from sunlight during the day (it was clear
that regular glass provided no such help).

Buffy's tombstone (when she died the second time), "She saved the
world . . . a lot."

Buffy even began a long-term romance with the vampire Angel, the
vampire with a soul. Angel was later spun off into his own series called
Angel. There he battled his inner demons as well as others that happened to be handy. Angel's adventures took him from the depths of the
Los Angeles sewers to its skyscraper heights, wrestling with modern life
along the way.

So where are vampires going
now? Increasingly, they are shed-
ding some age-old habits, such as
the fear of the sun or of religious
objects. In *Blade* (1998), Wesley
Snipes plays a vampire hunter who
is half-vampire himself. He wears a
futuristic costume and has the futuristic weapons to go with it. Is
this what lies ahead for vampires—

In most cultures, vampires were
people. But this wasn't a law.
For example, pumpkins that
got a little overripe could be
transformed. A pumpkin with
a jack-o'-lantern face is one
thing, but a pumpkin that moves
around, makes noises, and drips
blood is a whole lot worse.

In *Underworld* (2003), the vampire Selene (Kate Beckinsale, *center*) is caught in a war between vampires and werewolves.

a mingling of science fiction and traditional folk-lore? Purists may protest, but clearly vampires are as subject to change as anyone. The one constant they maintain, though, is their thirst for blood. Whatever else happens, they are not giving that up. And so whether vampires choose to live in cas-tle fortresses or behind the picket fence of the house next door, they will always bear watching. But don't get too close—you might not live to regret it!

Excerpt from Bram Stoker's *Dracula**

The novel *Dracula* begins as the diary of a young Englishman, Jonathan Harker. Harker is a lawyer traveling on business to meet a mysterious European nobleman, Count Dracula. On his way to Castle Dracula, Harker stops in a small village in Transylvania (in modern-day Romania). When the villagers learn that Harker is going to Castle Dracula, they're horrified. He shrugs off their fears as peasant superstitions—until he meets Count Dracula himself. In this passage, Harker describes his first evening with the count.

Dracula's face was a strong, a very strong, aquiline, with high bridge of the thin nose and peculiarly arched nostrils, with lofty domed forehead, and hair growing scantily round the temples but profusely elsewhere....The mouth, so far as I could see it under the heavy moustache, was fixed and rather cruel-looking, with peculiarly sharp white teeth....As the Count leaned over me and his hands touched me, I could not repress a shudder....A horrible feeling of nausea came over me, which, do what I would, I could not conceal.

The Count, evidently noticing it, drew back. And with a grim sort of smile...sat himself down again on his own side of the fireplace. We were both silent for a while, and as I looked towards the window I saw the first dim streak of the coming dawn. There seemed a strange stillness over everything. But as I listened, I heard as if from down below in the valley the howling of many wolves. The Count's eyes gleamed, and he said,

*"Listen to them, the children of the night. What music they make!"
Seeing, I suppose, some expression in my face strange to him, he
added, "Ah, sir, you dwellers in the city cannot enter into the feelings
of the hunter."*

Little does Harker suspect what—or who—Count Dracula hunts.
Even after realizing that he is a prisoner in Castle Dracula,
Harker cannot guess that Dracula's plans extend beyond him—to
England and Harker's innocent bride-to-be, Mina....

* Bram Stoker, *Dracula* (1897; repr., New York: Back Bay Books, 2005), 27–28.
Also available online at the Literature Network, http://www.literature.org/
authors/stoker-bram/dracula/, ch. 2 (September 2005).

SELECTED BIBLIOGRAPHY

Bunson, Matthew. *The Vampire Encyclopedia*. New York: Crown Publishing, 1994.

Dunn-Mascetti, Manuela. *Vampire: The Complete Guide to the World of the Undead*. New York: Viking, 1992.

Guiley, Rosemary Ellen. *The Encyclopedia of Vampires, Werewolves, and Other Monsters*. New York: Facts on File, Inc., 2005.

Halliwell, Leslie. *The Dead That Walk. Dracula, Frankenstein, the Mummy and Other Favorite Movie Monsters*. New York: Continuum Publishing, 1986.

McNally, Raymond T., and Radu Florescu. *In Search of Dracula: The History of Dracula and Vampires*. Boston: Houghton Mifflin, 1994.

Melton, J. Gordon. *The Vampire Book: The Encyclopedia of the Undead*. Detroit: Visible Ink Press, 1998.

Skal, David J. *Hollywood Gothic: The Tangled Web of Dracula from Novel to Stage to Screen*. New York: W.W. Norton & Company, 1990.

FURTHER READING AND WEBSITES

Allie, Scott, and Ben Abernathy, eds. *Buffy the Vampire Slayer: The Origin*. Milwaukie, OR: Dark Horse Comics, 1999. This graphic novel is based on the original Buffy movie script, updated to match the TV series. It traces the origin of the Slayer from medieval Europe to modern-day Los Angeles.

Dracula's Homepage

http://www.ucs.mun.ca/~emiller/

University lecturer Elizabeth Miller's site is a guide to Bram Stoker's

novel, its historical and mythical roots, and its influence on popular culture.

Hautman, Pete. *Sweetblood*. New York: Simon and Schuster, 2003. In this novel, sixteen-year-old Lucy spends most of her time trying to control her diabetes. And after Lucy develops a theory linking diabetes and vampirism, her fascination with vampires grows.

Polidori, John. *The Vampire*. Adapted by Les Martin. New York: Random House, 1989. Polidori's story "The Vampyre" is made available to younger readers in this adaptation.

Rooke, Sebastian. *Vampire Plagues*. New York: Scholastic Books, 2005. In this novel, Jack is a poor boy living on the streets of Victorian London. Then he meets Benedict, a boy his own age with a terrible tale to tell: a vampire invasion is under way. The boys vow to stop the vampires and solve the mystery of what really happened to Benedict's father.

Slonaker, Erin. *The Vampire Hunter's Handbook*. New York: Price Stern Sloan, 2001. This humorous guide offers practical advice on vampire hunting, such as where to find vampires, how to identify a real vampire, and how to protect yourself against one.

Stoker, Bram. *The Annotated Dracula*. Edited by Leonard Wolf. New York: Crown Publishing, 1975. This reprint of Stoker's classic novel includes maps, illustrations, and extensive comments by noted Dracula scholar Wolf.

Yolen, Jane, and Martin H. Greenberg, eds. *Vampires*. New York: Harper Trophy, 1991. This collection of twelve original vampire stories for middle-grade readers includes humor and horror.

MOVIES AND TV

Buffy the Vampire Slayer. Los Angeles: Twentieth Century Fox Home Video, 2004. DVD. This 1992 movie first brought vampires to the suburbs. It stars Kristy Swanson, Luke Perry, and Hilary Swank.

Buffy the Vampire Slayer. Los Angeles: Twentieth Century Fox Home Video, 2002–2004. DVD. This collection includes all seven seasons of the popular TV show starring Sarah Michelle Gellar, David Boreanaz, and Alyson Hannigan.

Dracula. Universal City, CA: Universal Studios, 2001. DVD. The DVD of the 1931 classic starring Bela Lugosi includes a documentary on the making of the movie. Also included is a commentary track by vampire and Dracula expert David J. Skal.

Lost Boys. Burbank, CA: Warner Home Video, 2004. DVD. After their parents' divorce, two brothers (played by Jason Patric and Corey Haim) move with their mom to a new town. They soon begin to suspect that a group of vampires haunts the area. The two-disc DVD edition includes a documentary on the making of the movie.

Nosferatu. Chatsworth, CA: Image Entertainment, 2002. DVD. The restored special edition DVD of the 1922 silent movie highlights director F. W. Murnau's innovative camera work and Max Schreck's eerie performance as the title vampire.

INDEX

ABOUT THE AUTHOR

Stephen Krensky is the author of many fiction and nonfiction books for children, including titles in the On My Own Folklore series and *Frankenstein*, *Werewolves*, *Dragons*, *The Mummy*, and *Bigfoot*. When he isn't hunched over his computer, he makes school visits and teaches writing workshops. In his free time, he enjoys playing tennis and softball and reading books by other people. Krensky lives in Massachusetts with his wife, Joan, and their family.

PHOTO ACKNOWLEDGMENTS

The images in this book are used with the permission of: © Criswell/The Kobal Collection, p. 2–3; Victoria & Albert Museum, London/Art Resource, NY, p. 9; © Bettmann/CORBIS, pp. 10, 25, 29; © Richard Cummins/SuperStock, p. 11; © Gunter Ziesler/Peter Arnold, Inc., p. 14; *Bram Stoker's Dracula*, © 1992 Columbia Pictures Industries, Inc., All Rights Reserved. Courtesy of Columbia Pictures, pp. 15 (image provided by © Everett Collection), 31; Supplied by CP-Globe Photos, p. 16; © Dennis Báthory-Kitsz, http://bathory.org, p. 21; © National Portrait Gallery/SuperStock, p. 23; © Erich Lessing/Art Resource, NY, p. 26; Courtesy of Universal Studios Licensing LLLP, p. 27; © Everett Collection, pp. 30, 34; © CBS-TV/The Kobal Collection, p. 35; © Tricia Meadows/Globe Photos, p. 36; *Interview with the Vampire*, © Geffen Pictures. Licensed by Warner Bros. Entertainment, Inc. All Rights Reserved, p. 37; *Buffy the Vampire Slayer*, © 1992 Twentieth Century Fox. All rights reserved, p. 38; *Buffy the Vampire Slayer*, © 2003 Twentieth Century Fox Television. All rights reserved, p. 39; Permission courtesy of Sony Home Entertainment, image provided by Photofest, Inc., p. 41; Illustrations by Bill Hauser, 1, 6–7, 8, 10–13, 18–19, 20, 24, 33. All page backgrounds illustrated by Bill Hauser/Independent Picture Service.

Cover illustration by Bill Hauser